Make The World Your Oyster!

Make The World Your Oyster!

___

Adventuring beyond your Comfort Zone

Michael Lum Y.M.

Foreword by **Stephen C. Lundin**, Ph.D
Author of the five million copy best-selling: **FISH!**

———

Make The World Your Oyster!

———

terra es mea ocystae

———

"Why, then the world's mine oyster,
Which I with sword will open."

Pistol to Falstaff
The Merry Wives of Windsor
William Shakespeare

———

ISBN: 1511626143
ISBN 13: 9781511626149
Library of Congress Control Number: 2015912503
CreateSpace Independent Publishing Platform
North Charleston, South Carolina

Foreword

Once upon a time, in a faraway land, a frog went for a stroll in the forest. Enjoying the day but not paying attention, he lost his way. As night approached, he sought shelter and as luck would have it, he chanced upon a cottage. *How fortunate*, he thought. Finding no one home, he looked for a place to rest. In the kitchen, his luck continued when he found a pot of warm water. *Heaven*, he thought as he relaxed into it. What he did not know is that the owner of the home had set the pot on the stove to boil and then gone out to collect additional firewood. The water became warmer and he grew sleepy, fell asleep and was boiled alive.

This story is told in a variety of forms all over the world. I am told that a frog would actually jump out before it got boiled. Such details do not detract from the fundamental truth the story contains. When we get too relaxed and comfortable with the status quo and stop growing, we are at risk of falling behind. It is rare for an organization or person to maintain static form. As the saying goes, "grow or die."

In the last five years, the world has witnessed so many changes – the Internet, search engines, social media, business connectivity, e-books, online education, instant messaging, tablets, mobile communication devices, budget airlines, eco-products, bio-engineering, designer genes, etc. It is imperative that we adapt and innovate.

What is a comfort zone? What is normal for you? As someone based in the US, I have learned that when travelling to London or Sydney, my life is at risk. Why? Because I look the wrong way when crossing the street! To stay safe, I need to adjust and unfortunately, that usually results in rapid oscillation of the head at the curb because I know there is danger but have not yet developed a new habit.

In Wikipedia, comfort zone is defined this way: a behavioral state within which a person operates in an <u>anxiety</u>-neutral condition, using a limited set of behaviors to deliver a steady level of performance, usually without a sense of <u>risk</u>. We create our own comfortable logic bubbles and become contented in them. Should life force us out for a moment, we scramble back as soon as we can. Yet research shows that the best performance occurs when we are stretched to our limits but not beyond.

I love stories and obviously favor animals with books titled FISH! and CATS. Make The World Your Oyster! is an illuminating business parable about two dolphins who are mid-life executives. As their products reach the end of the life cycle, they ponder their situation. In the quest for solutions, they have a series of adventures containing both surprise and wisdom.

Michael Lum is a consummate storyteller whom I have known for some time. He is passionate about his work and the role of stories as teaching tools. This parable reflects precisely the realities of today's corporate world to which we must respond or be left behind. As you read this book, put yourself in the story and consider the decisions you have to make and the consequences of those decisions.

Used in the right way, this book will guide you out of your comfort zone and into the innovation zone.

Make The World Your Oyster! Go and search for the pearl.

Stephen C. Lundin, Ph.D

Author of the five million copy best-selling:
FISH! A Remarkable Way to Boost Morale and Improve Performance (12 Years Number 1 in Customer Service)

Other books include FISH! Sticks, FISH! Tales, FISH! for Life Top Performer, Loops, CATS: The Nine Lives of Innovation and Ubuntu: An Inspiring Story about an African Tradition of Teamwork and Collaboration

———

I

"Turn it off!"

"Who was that numbskull who invented the alarm clock?"

The alarm sprang to life as the clock struck five past six.

"I need at least eight hours of sleep…"

Sensing no action, Status Quo grabbed the clock and slammed it down. Silence followed immediately.

"Wake up, Status Quo! If we are late again, we'll be dead fish," warned Ventura with a touch of brotherly concern.

"Oh, no. Work again… We'll die from work very soon."

The morning was dim and sluggish. The coconut leaves danced daintily as a light breeze strolled across. Wave after wave unfolded their gathers as they rolled onto the shore. Their velocity was significantly reduced by friction as they rubbed against the sand. As each wave lost its momentum, it retreated obediently into the sea. In the far horizon, the sun rose sheepishly. It gave light to dawn so that day could arrive. Its golden rays peeped shyly through the coconut leaves onto the shores as if it was a solar clock reminding the marine creatures to awaken to the new day. Slowly but surely, the sun threw its increasingly resplendent rays on Dolphinarium, a major tourist attraction in an idyllic seaside resort called Exista, located by the Red Sea in a country called New Workland.

Dolphinarium, the award-winning six-star tourist destination, featured stellar performances by a wide cast of marine animals. Its USP (Unique Selling Proposition) was a world-class marine animal show, which drew strong praise despite equally strong opposition from WETMA (World for Ethical Treatment of Marine Animals).

In the show, marine animals were trained to perform dangerous stunts on aquabikes, speedboats and surfboards, and kept in confined environments.

"Every company in town is stating the obvious," sighed Status Quo as they passed the entrance of Dolphinarium.

"Well, there's a certain amount of truth in it!" exclaimed Ventura.

There was a gigantic billboard welcoming the guests:

You, The Customers are the King and the Queen.
You are the only reason we are still here.

The majority of Dolphinarium's shares were owned by Hammerhead Shark and his family. He was revered as a hard-headed businessman and a tough negotiator. Always wary of competition, he guarded his turf well by stamping out all possible competitors or erecting high barriers of entry. He could do so by virtue of his position as the Chairman of ATARS (Association of Tourist Attractions in Red Sea). A seasoned businessman, he would impose new rules and regulations specifically for his own advantage. Always seen in his signature white suit, he was a charismatic boss with an imposing figure. He ruled Dolphinarium with an iron fist gloved in velvet. To say the least, his leadership style was autocratic. Some swore it was dictatorial.

His motto was cheekily scribbled across the blackboard in the conference room:

My Way or the Highway

Those who dared to oppose him fell by the wayside. His employees — dolphins, killer whales and seals — always nodded their heads and replied, "Yes Sir!" No one dared to sail close to the wind, raise any questions or challenge his decisions.

Ventura and Status Quo Dolphina were four-year-old, 12-foot-long, playful and intelligent grayish bottlenose dolphins. The siblings were born and raised in captivity at Dolphinarium. Their backs were dark gray while their bellies were of lighter gray. From afar, they could be identified by their grayish curved dorsal fins. Mama and Papa were captured in a purse-seine net by fishermen who then sold them to Dolphinarium. Over the years, they had been domesticated and trained to be performers, entertaining tourists flying in from all corners of the world.

As the limited space and artificial environment were not conducive for dolphins to mate and conceive, Ventura and Status Quo had been the products of artificial insemination. Chips of the old block, it was only natural for them to follow Mama and Papa into show business. They had lived a fairly sheltered life, especially for the first three years when Mama nursed them till puberty. As a result, they used little of their mammalian instincts in navigation, foraging and avoiding predators.

From a tender age, they had been trained to perform aquatic stunts and deliver performances at a level that exceeded customer expectations. The spectators, especially children, applauded their spectacular performance — high jumping into loops lined with knives and lit with fire, leaping to reach for high balls suspended by high wire, acrobatically somersaulting and synchronized swimming. In one sequence, a performer in a wetsuit would put one leg on each of their backs as they surfed through the waters. In the next set, the performer would ride on Ventura's back holding only onto his dorsal fin. Other acts involved aqua-bikes, speedboats and surfboards. Wow! The children simply adored it!

The dolphins clicked and squeaked with their elongated upper jaws and shorter lower jaws. Then, they whistled from their blowholes on top of their heads. Midway through the performance, Ventura and Status Quo would swim dangerously close to the audience and suddenly spring up high, somersault with a three-quarter turn and do a freefall, splashing water on spectators in the splash zone — the first 12 rows.

The most popular act was tail-walking where they held their bodies vertically out of the water and moved backwards by thrashing their tails. Next came tail-slapping, in which they used their tails to hit the water surface rhythmically according to the beat of the song, *The Champions in Us*. Another popular performance had Status Quo piggybacking on her brother, Ventura and rolling just beneath the water. There were always *oohs* and *aahs* from the spectators. As they completed their final performance, they would wave goodbye with their pectoral fins and surprise the audience by beaching themselves onto a platform right in front of them, with their tails saluting in the air. The audience was wowed every time.

When they executed their acts successfully, the trainers patted their heads and exclaimed, "Well done!", rewarding them with herring, cod or mackerel. It was just another day at work.

As quota carriers, Ventura and Status Quo were incentivized to hit their targets with monetary rewards like annual increments and bonuses, or non-monetary ones like recognition or days off.

"Things are not all that rosy. When we fail to perform up to the specified standards, we're punished by limited food supply and solitary confinement. Sometimes, we're deprived of adequate hours of sleep. This is essentially the cane and carrot style of motivation — punishment for poor performance and rewards for a job well done," explained Ventura to some of his friends.

"Our KPI (Key Performance Indicators) are the gate-takings and the applause of the audience. Appraisals are conducted weekly. Letters of praise and brickbats are evaluated, too. At times we inflate our scores by asking our friends to put in some kind words," added Status Quo.

II

"I see these statements screaming at me so often I can repeat them backwards!" exclaimed Status Quo.

"Every company just blindly follows one another," sighed Ventura.

The entrance to Dolphinarium was adorned with marble sculptures of marine creatures. The statements decked the walls of the reception:

Vision

To be the most unforgettable six-star tourist destination, delighting customers with unique world-class experiences

Mission

To create ultimate joy for our customers by continually challenging the frontiers of technology and innovation in marine entertainment

Corporate Values

1. Our customers are kings and queens. We deliver the best service value and customer experience, exceeding their expectations. Always.
2. We endeavor to deliver the most innovative entertainment products to our customers.
3. Our staff is our best asset. We value them and their contributions highly. We create a stimulating work environment to realize their fullest potential.
4. We respect and care for the environment. We are responsible corporate citizens.
5. We seek maximum value for our stakeholders and reinvest both in product and technology to achieve continuous growth.

Every employee carried a laminated pocket card spelling out four daily affirmations. Every time they opened their wallets, these affirmations stared at them.

Daily Affirmations

1. We work with a fighting spirit. "Never Quit" is our mantra.
2. We collaborate with each other to compete against others in the marketplace.
3. We demonstrate empathy towards our co-workers.
4. We strive for continuous learning and innovation in our work.

Employees in Dolphinarium viewed these statements as necessary corporate embellishment. They were nice-to-have positive reinforcement that no one took seriously. Many corporations worth their salt also had similar corporate statements hanging prettily on the walls of their reception.

To inspire its staff to greater heights, the Dolphinarium management hung motivational posters in the canteen, corridors and its main office.

WORK is G.R.E.A.T!
Getting Really Enthusiastic About Today!

T.E.A.M.
Today, Executives Are Motivated

T.E.A.M. Works
Together, Everyone Achieves More

P.R.I.D.E.
Proud and Responsible In Delivering Excellence

F.O.R.C.E.
Focus On Reducing Costs Everywhere

S.U.C.C.E.S.S.
Without U, there's no Success!

Be the Best,
Ignore the Rest!

Customers are our Paymasters.
They put food on our tables.

Make lemonade out of lemons,
Find opportunity in every adversity.

There's No Failure;
Only Success Delayed

Since birth, the only world known to Ventura and Status Quo was the grounds of Dolphinarium — a 9-hectare area consisting of a huge 2,888-seat horseshoe amphitheater, a practice pool, medical center, burger fast-food outlet, coffee joint, gift shop, administration building and two restaurants, one serving Chinese Szechuan cuisine and the other French.

Why 2,888 seats? Well, Hammerhead Shark was a great believer in *fengshui*. Leaving nothing to chance, he had consulted Lu Kong, a *fengshui* grandmaster, on the design of Dolphinarium.

"Red features prominently as it is a lucky color. To collect positive *chi*, it is shaped like a horseshoe facing south. The numbers '2888' symbolize good fortune to the Chinese because they sound like 'easy to prosper progressively' in Cantonese. An upright horseshoe ensures good luck is contained within it and will not spill out. For the best *fengshui*, it faces south to avoid both the direct sun and to capture the North-South wind," Lu Kong from Hong Kong explained.

"Every day is routine. Either we rest in their quarters, practice in the pool or perform in the amphitheater. As performers, we have been indoctrinated to win applause from the audience. The higher the attendance and the more applause we receive from the audience, the better rated is our performance," complained Status Quo.

Another gauge of their performance was the revenue from the gift shops and tour groups. If the audience were impressed with the performance, they would buy a souvenir or two. Similarly, if inbound tour operators were impressed with the performance, they would recommend other tour groups. So every day, the dolphins performed, come rain or shine. Well, except for Monday, their rest day. Such was the routine of show business.

In their quarters, sheets of papers were pinned on the notice board to serve as a constant reminder for their work.

Weekly Goals
Set targets higher than the moon.
If you fail, you can still fall on the stars.

100% Attendance in Training
100% Attendance in Shows
Above 90% Rating in Performance

Grab more than what you need because some will spill.

Daily Schedule
Follow your timetable
and there'll be food on your table.

6.00 am	**Rise and Shine**
6.30 am	**Training Session**
9.00 am	**Breakfast**
10.00 am	**Morning Show**
12.00 pm	**Lunch**
2.00 pm	**Rest**
3.00 pm	**Afternoon Show**
6.00 pm	**Dinner**
7.00 pm	**Free Time**
10.00 pm	**Lights Out**

Procrastination robs both your time and bank account.

III

"Do you realize our whole world revolves around Dolphinarium? It's well-structured and organized hierarchically. Everything we do, in one way or another, is result-oriented. Since birth, we have never left its grounds. We don't have a clue what lies beyond its boundaries," grumbled Ventura.

The confined pool, with its stale water and warm temperature, was inadequate for them to develop themselves to their fullest potential. Insufficient stimulation, to say the least.

Occasionally, Ventura looked up to see a golden eagle soaring across the blue skies. It glided so effortlessly, surveying everyone below.

"What is it? Where does it come from? Where will it go? How does it fly so high? Could dolphins fly, too? But all we know to do is swim, leap and dive to the applause of the audience," wondered Ventura.

Besides Dolphinarium, Exista was dotted with tourist attractions to lure the tourist dollar. The main customers were the Chinese, Japanese, Americans and Europeans. Tourist attractions included Movie Splendor, which screened high-definition 360-degree movies; The Titanic, a re-creation of the world's once biggest and unsinkable ocean liner; Fantasia Island, a pirate adventure cove; and Cartoons Alive!, a theme park featuring cartoon characters from the movies.

There were three giant casinos — Golden Nuggets, El Dorado and Cleopatra. There were also mega shopping centers, opulent luxury brand retail outlets and five-star hotels with their two-star Michelin restaurants and entertainment outlets.

Business at Dolphinarium was brisk. Within a few years of setting up, Dolphinarium had established its brand and its fame spread far and wide. It was on every person's bucket list, to visit Dolphinarium at least once in their lifetime. Its success bred competition. Two years later, another giant aquatic attraction complete with sea animals muscled in. Named after the lost city of Atlantis, it was 60 percent larger than Dolphinarium and featured more state-of-the-art and adrenaline-rushing attractions.

"The grapevine has it that another big boy is planning an attraction of an even larger scale that could revolutionize the entertainment world. It's called Tidal Wave," whispered Ventura.

"I heard the crocodiles don't want to miss the boat. They want to model Dolphinarium's and build Crocodilarium, billed as the only attraction of its kind in the world. All the performers are crocodiles and alligators of different shapes and sizes. You can even swim in an enclosed iron cage dipped into the same pool as the killer crocs and experience some of the most terrifying moments of your life," added Status Quo.

The Exista Town Council subscribed to economies of scale and the law of numbers. The more attractions it had, the more easily they could justify building more infrastructure, and at a lower cost. The more attractions Exista had, the more tourists it could attract.

Soon, Red Sea turned very competitive. The marketplace got crowded. Tourist attractions had no qualms about slashing their prices to stay afloat. They incurred heavy advertising expenses and launched aggressive marketing campaigns to entice customers. The acquisition costs to secure new customers and retention costs to retain old ones ballooned. Stealing customers from other attractions and making them stay longer at their own attraction was the order of the day. That was the main avenue to increase their revenue from a fixed pie. The tourists were spoilt for choice.

Everyone spied on and analyzed their competitors' performance. Whenever one business performed well, others would duplicate its winning formula in no time. Copycats abounded. No matter how much they differentiated their products and services, there was a limit on what they could do. Brand differentiation was a difficult act to perfect. Products and services degenerated into commodities. Profit margins shrunk rapidly.

War was declared. All hell broke loose. The big fish devoured the small fish. There was a bloodbath in the Red Sea. Blood was shed daily. Many businesses bit the dust as a result of intense cut-throat competition.

"Our customers have been fast dwindling. For years, the directors and I have been cracking our heads to reinvent ourselves. We hired top-notch Wall Street consultancy firms staffed with Ivy League graduates to help us think laterally, pioneer out-of-the-box innovation initiatives and launch aggressive strategic plans. We even tried to hire wild animals like polar bears and sharks. The success, however, has been short-lived. To contain costs, we have to retrench some workers and downsize our operations. We seek your understanding," explained Hammerhead Shark in a downsizing exercise.

"We are the first to be kicked out," cried the older killer whales who knew they were slow and clumsy. Being the largest performers, they occupied the most workspace and were the most costly to maintain.

Ventura and Status Quo were trapped in the throes of their mid-life crisis. They were bored to death by the daily humdrum of work. Although they were tired of entertaining, they needed a job to pay their bills. Jobs, however, were hard to come by, as there were limited attractions that would employ dolphins as entertainers. The siblings were aware they had to leave their comfort zone to remain relevant with the times.

"Have you ever spared a thought on what would happen when we grow old?" asked Ventura.

"Sorry. Never," replied Status Quo.

"Never thought about it?"

"Well, I take one day at a time. I live for the moment."

"The future frightens me. The day will come when we're no longer useful to Dolphinarium — when we can't leap as high, can't swim as fast and can't dive as deep as now. Then they'll dump us and hire newer and younger dolphins. The sell-by date will come in the blink of an eye. What if we are injured? Heaven forbid. They would retire us immediately."

"Well, I can't afford to worry too much. Many have the 'monkey mind', worrying about one issue after another. We don't know what tomorrow will bring. I believe in the power of the *here and now*," replied Status Quo as she looked down dejectedly.

Ventura gave her a perplexed look, "Companies are downsizing, rightsizing and capsizing."

"Admittedly, thoughts of the future do cross my mind occasionally. But I practice the Zen technique of pushing these fleeting thoughts gently away and focusing only on today. It's called Mindfulness. Many have their minds full of anger and worries. The past is gone and buried in history. Your worries about the future may not materialize. Only today is a reality you can work on. Worries don't reduce the size of the problem."

"I look towards the future — through scenario planning. It's a mind opener to paint different scenarios and have a preview of what the future may hold. Applying Kurt Lewin's Force Field Analysis is stimulating - the driving and restraining forces that settle into an equilibrium," cautioned Ventura.

"That is too technical, Ventura. Scenario planning, driving forces, restraining forces, and whatnots. For all you know, the scenarios you plan for may not happen."

"Well, we can hope for the best and prepare for the worst. After all, Murphy's Law states that what can go wrong, will go wrong. Things go wrong at the most critical moment."

Being the more adventurous and ambitious of the two, Ventura went hunting for a job. He applied for a few jobs advertised in the newspapers. He surfed the net and alerted the headhunters of his intention. Five months later, his efforts bore fruits. Through a recruitment outfit, he secured a job as a performer in a riverboat restaurant, Sunset Diners, which specialized in barbecued seafood. The job description required him to perform a song and dance routine while diners barbecued their seafood and watched the glorious sun bid farewell in resplendent golden hues.

"Shall I resign? Shall I accept new challenges? Shall I have a change of environment?" He pondered. There were many questions popping into his head. It was an internal struggle. Only time would tell if he was making the right decision.

Decision. Decision. Decision.

After three days of insightful reflection, Ventura tendered his resignation, giving three months' notice. He was delighted to note that competition clauses were absent in his employment contract. Although he had two months of leave left, he could not commence work in a month's time as it was illegal to work during his garden leave.

Sunset Diners was located near the mouth of Black River, where it flowed into the Dead Sea. It was 31 miles west from the Red Sea. A few attractions were littered along Black River. It was a slow, muddy river that meandered through sparse vegetation. This was a result of large-scale irrigation. There was not much life here. Sunset Diners' main strength lay in its cozy and personalized dining experience. The owners believed that a dolphin show would value-add to their customers' unforgettable experience as they dined. To save costs, Ventura was a one-man band. Business gradually picked up with the dolphin show.

Nine months later, the boss of Sunset Diners informed Ventura, "The government has announced they are building a dam in Black River to generate hydro-electricity. A dam ensures only a trickle of water will seep into the Dead Sea. It will make the Dead Sea even more stagnant. As it is, due to its high salinity and the harsh weather, the Dead Sea is bereft of marine life and aquatic plants. Even its shores are devoid of shrubs and trees."

Construction activities brought a slow, painful death to businesses along Black River. Pollution, noise and heavy machineries deterred tourists from visiting the place. Businesses could not justify their existence. All the establishments by the Dead Sea hurriedly announced plans to relocate to other parts of New Workland. Soon, residents nicknamed the delta of Black River "Ghost Town".

True to its name, Sunset Diners soon bit the dust. Ventura was retrenched. Other businesses like motels, restaurants and country resorts also closed their doors. The owner of Sunset Diners regretted choosing a river that led to a "dead sea". As the years were catching up on him, Ventura grew more tired of performing to exacting standards all the time. He was burnt out.

He caught up with Status Quo to pour out his pent-up frustrations.

"I'm unemployed now. I have to update my resume and scout for another job," Ventura said, feeling a tinge of regret about leaving Dolphinarium.

Lending a pair of empathetic ears, Status Quo advised, "You can always speak to Executo. I'm sure Dolphinarium will welcome you back. After all, you were a loyal and outstanding employee."

Egged on by Status Quo, Ventura made an appointment with Executo, the HR director of Dolphinarium, with the hope of being re-instated at his old job. He was glad that he had not burnt any bridges when he left.

"I'm sorry," Executo explained, "Dolphinarium is barely covering its costs. We cannot afford to hire another performer, especially one with your premium package. Besides, as you may be aware, you are past your prime. I acknowledge you were a loyal and diligent worker. All I can say is 'Thank you. I wish you all the best in your future endeavors'. I'll buy you a cuppa the next time we meet."

Although Executo was being diplomatic in concluding the meeting with an invitation to coffee, Ventura sensed his insincerity.

To say he was dejected was an understatement. Many a time he would loiter outside Dolphinarium. He would peep in at the performance where he was once the prima donna — the star performer of the show. He would listen, with guarded jealousy, to the applause that was once reserved for him. However, those were his past glories. Would they be repeated in the near future? Or would they be etched in the memories of history?

IV

Unemployed and with plenty of time to kill, Ventura attended a few previews of motivational courses. This was the first time he had attended such talks. He never knew that such courses existed, let alone that he needed to attend one. After all, he was an alpha male and indestructible — once upon a time. To prevent embarrassing himself when other participants asked what he did for a living, he printed calling cards designating himself as a principal consultant   a euphemism for highly-qualified unemployed professionals.

To upgrade himself, he reasoned that he had to take action by investing in one of these courses. So he invested in one program which he thought was the most appropriate — *Wake Up the Genius Inside* by a rah-rah American motivational guru, Ian Mulekim. He was touted as The Pearl Finder of Pacific – he had helped many participants locate the forgotten pearls in their lives. To benefit fully from the workshop, Ventura put aside his preconceived notions and was all ears.

He thought, "Why didn't I attend these courses earlier? Why didn't Dolphinarium upgrade me through such courses? In my heyday, I slogged my guts out without thinking about my future. I should have planned for a second career – a Plan B. I should have known I can't be jumping up and down once I've passed my prime."

On the first day of the course, all participants were advised to participate with an open mind. Mulekim wrote:

An open mind is like a parachute. If it's closed, it's deadly.

Later, everyone had the entire morning to answer the question:

Who is the bus driver?

(Spend one minute thinking about the answer.)

The answer is:

I am.

Mulekim delivered this message with evangelical fervor, "Do not let anyone drive the bus of your life. You will be at their mercy. Take charge of your own life. Drive the bus of your life yourself. If another person is the driver, your life is in jeopardy. He may lose control, turn turtle or worse, crash into a ravine."

After lunch, Mulekim preached affirmation and self-limiting beliefs passionately.

Every hour, the participants parroted self-affirmation statements and auto-suggested themselves to attain peak condition. They flexed their pectoral fins and beat their chests as they yelled:

I am great!
I am fine!
I'm this way all the time!

Each participant wrote his or her self-limiting beliefs on a slab of wood. Some of these were:

I am too young to start a business.
I am too old to start a business.
I don't have sufficient capital.
I don't have a degree.
I am not gifted.
I don't have enough energy.
I don't come from a rich family.
I am a woman.
I can fail.
Everything was easier in the past.
There are insufficient business opportunities.
The market here is too small.

They then smashed the slabs up with their snouts — a powerful metaphor for destroying their self-limiting beliefs. Now, they were ready to meet new challenges head-on without the baggage of yesteryears.

In the morning of the second day, the participants had to answer another question:

Am I the cause or the effect?

(Spend one minute thinking about the answer.)

The answer is:

I am the cause.

Mulekim preached passionately, "You are the sum effect of all your previous causes. Now you must become the cause of the effects in your life. Take initiative to make things happen. If others are the cause, you are at the receiving end of things that happen. You have no control whatsoever over your life. Take charge of your life now. Chart your direction — What do you want to do? Where do you want to go? In other words, you must be 'proactive' instead of 'reactive'."

C > E

"The cause must be larger than the effect. This is karma. When there is an effect, there must be a cause. In other words, the cause makes the effect happen. You sow the seeds; you reap the fruit. There will be no harvest if no seeds have been planted. If you plant tomato seeds, you won't harvest potatoes tomorrow. To put it plainly: You reap what you sow. Nothing happens without a cause."

Ventura declared insightfully, "This is an AHA moment!"

In the morning of the third day, they learned:

Perception is projection.

Mulekim continued to dispense his words of wisdom, "Whatever you perceive in your mind, you project and manifest it outwardly. If you are nervous about giving a presentation in public, the audience sees anxiety written all over your face. If you are shy about meeting strangers at a function, guests can sense your shyness. Whatever is in your mind will be reflected in your physical behavior. The body never lies. Perception is reality."

According to body language expert Albert Mehrabian, a Professor Emeritus of Psychology at UCLA, three elements account for why we like a person: words (7%), tone of voice (38%), and body language (55%). These are often abbreviated as the "3 Vs" — Verbal, Vocal and Visual. In other words, non-verbal language comprises a massive 93%. This was confirmed in a seminal study by Professor Ray Birdwhistell, who concluded that 65% of face-to-face communication was non-verbal and 35% verbal.

"Let's be MAD!" screamed Mulekim suddenly at the top of his voice. "To change our lives, we must be MAD at our own selves. To change the world, we should be MAD at other people."

Ventura and the other participants were shell-shocked for a minute, "Why should we go berserk?" Towards tea-break, the speaker finally revealed what the acronym M.A.D. stood for.

M.A.D.
Make A Difference

"I must make a difference in my life today," Ventura swore.

V

After the program, Ventura mustered enough courage and gathered
more momentum to create a compelling future for himself. He had
to MAD (make a difference) in his own life by becoming the bus
driver first. He wanted to be the cause — implement his entrepre-
neurial skills. Naming his company Dolphina Tours, he planned to
provide in-bound tours to tourists using a chartered boat. Ventura
wanted to give it a try. Perhaps he would have beginner's luck. He
reflected on why he had not started a business earlier and composed
a poem:

If only
If only I gossip less,
If only I harbor less fear,
If only I have less worries,
If only I am less emotional,
If only I watch less TV,
If only I am more courageous,
If only I had done things earlier,
If only I forsake the comfort zone,
If only I engage in less frivolous activities,
If only I have more initiative,
If only I am more decisive,
If only I procrastinate less,
If only I am more patient,

If only I am more driven,
If only I am more focused,
If only I learn more,
If only I listen more to my heart,
What would the results be?

Business was both slow and competitive. Ventura was stressed. Still, he thought that venturing into some business was better than being unemployed, staying at home and causing his self-esteem to plunge. It was the only way to keep himself sane. During certain lull periods, there were no tourists at all. To keep his business afloat, he dipped into his savings. Very soon, his savings sank to an all-time low. It was easy to start a business. To maintain it was another challenge. Highly-strung and depressed, he called it quits.

Jobless again, he wandered aimlessly in the Red Sea, like a vagabond. He asked himself, "Why me, of all people? Why didn't I succeed as an employee? Why didn't I succeed in business? Why are others so lucky? My God, why did I fail?"

In his failings, Ventura philosophized stoically to himself, "There is a season and reason for everything. It could be fated. It could be in the alignment of the stars when I was born. It could be my retribution. I could even be bearing the karmic sins of my forefathers."

The Maker above had a plan for him. Ventura now placed more emphasis on intangible things — contentment, health, friends and family. He practiced non-attachment. Silent contemplation was his catharsis. Transcendental meditation assumed the place of release valve for his pressures. Everything in the world was temporal.

He thought, "You cannot hold on to 'things' for long. When you are recalled by the Maker, you cannot bring all your riches with you. Naked you came into this world; naked you depart."

He recalled vaguely reading a verse in the Bible some time ago. "Do not accumulate treasures here on earth where moths eat and rust ruins them. Thieves can also break in and steal them."

As Ventura looked up into the sky, it reminded him of a line in Julius Caesar, "The fault is not in the stars."

He chanced upon the golden eagle again and thought, "How gracefully and effortlessly it slices through the skies. Such a vast expanse of blue skies in contrast to the limited stale waters of the Red Sea! How I wish I could soar like the eagle and rule the skies..."

His thinking went into overdrive. "Could there only be the Red Sea and the Dead Sea? What lies beyond? If only I can soar like the eagle, then my questions would be answered. Unfortunately, dolphins cannot fly."

One day during his aimless loitering to kill time, Ventura bumped into his old colleague, Applica, who was fired after seven months with his new employer. Together, they sulked and bemoaned the current state of affairs. Misery loves companionship. Together, they poured out their sorrows and commiserated. Out they went hunting for jobs but it was not easy. The whales grabbed many of the vacancies while the sharks were very aggressive, shoving and threatening the other applicants. Only the minnows soaked up all the low-paying short-term assignments.

"Surely we cannot mourn every day. Things will not change if we do not initiate any action. Let's venture beyond the shores of the Red Sea," reasoned Ventura, now more realistic and mature in his thoughts.

"Unless I leave the shores of comfort, I can never explore the ocean of opportunity."

Having nothing to lose, Applica agreed to try. After all, staying at home was boring and depressing. It did nothing to help the soul.

Together, Ventura and Applica set forth to new grounds. They headed south and met a new waterway, Yellow River. As they swam upstream, the stench became increasingly pungent. The waters were filled with rubbish, flotsam and greenish yellow chemicals discharged by the factories located further upstream. There was no proper disposal of waste. Everyone simply dumped waste conveniently into the river, without regard for the environment. It was the fastest and cheapest way.

It was filthy. Ventura and Applica could hardly breathe. They soon abandoned their dreams of landing jobs in the Yellow River.

"We must not give up. We must soldier on," Ventura assured himself as he tapped his chest.

As if to declare to the world their resolve, the two dolphins scribbled the following on a rock by Black River:

Leaders do not quit.
Quitters do not lead.

"Yes. You're right. Winners persist," agreed Applica, adding another two quotable quotes on the next rock:

Winners do things
losers dare not do.

Winners do not work on different things;
They work on things differently.

"What shall we do then?"

"Let's adopt The Contrarian Principle," suggested Applica.

"What is that?"

"Animals have the herd instinct. They follow the masses just like in migration during winter. The Contrarian Principle suggests you do the opposite of what the majority do. Let's venture further up north," suggested Ventura.

"Brilliant! I say 'No' to group think, too."

VI

Together, they leaped and dived towards the north-east of the Red Sea. Eager were they to know what lay beyond. They frolicked and foraged as they headed in a north-easterly direction.

After an hour, they came to a cul-de-sac. They could not see what was beyond the land, apart from rocks and some sturdy bushes.

They loitered to kill time.

Then, they heard something in the background.

What was it?

They strained their ears to identify the sound.

Yes, there was definitely something.

It was the faint roaring of waves.

Again, they strained their ears, located on both sides of their heads. They listened intently. They squinted their eyes and focused.

It was the roar of the sea waves and their crashing as they hit, presumably, the rocks. Now, the pair were convinced that something existed beyond this strip of land.

Something was indeed there. Snow-white seagulls and blackhead terns were frequently squawking and fluttering to and from a mysterious place. There appeared to be a hive of activity over yonder.

As eager as they were to find out what lay beyond, there was nothing much they could do. But the spirit of adventure and curiosity sustained their interest.

Having swum in the sea the entire day, Ventura looked up into the sky to rest his eyes. It dawned upon him that if someone knew what lay on the other side, it would be the golden eagle with a bird's eye view of the universe. He was the only one who had the answer. But the eagle was always high and aloof up in the sky. He pondered, "How can I seek his help?"

One misty morning, the eagle seemed to be descending very fast. It was like a falling star in the day. Ventura followed it. It was free-falling. It seemed like a falling kite when its line was cut. It was heading for the trees.

As it was about to land, two legs protruded and two flapping wings brought it to a screeching halt upon an old cypress tree on an outcrop.

It was not a golden eagle.

It was a white-belly osprey. With a fish in its beak, it was ready to consume its meal.

Jumping at the opportunity, Ventura asked, "Best morning. I'm glad to see you. How are you?"

"I'm very well. Thank you," replied the osprey as it devoured its catch.

"I'm so envious of you. You soar in the skies so effortlessly. It appears the whole sky belongs to you," praised Ventura in an attempt to gain favor in an answer.

"I marvel at you. You can dive to the depths of the sea and explore all its mysteries while I can only survey the beach."

Ventura took a guilt trip for not recognizing his own strengths. "Is the osprey aware that I can stay submerged in water for a maximum of only 20 minutes?" he thought.

"May I request a favor?"

"I attempt at least one good deed a day. If I can assist, it would be my pleasure," replied the osprey.

"Pray tell me, what lies beyond this sea? I can hear the faint crashing of waves in the distance."

"Oh. You mean you don't know?"

"Of course not. We are all trapped in this Red Sea. How would we know?"

"Oh, yes. Pardon me. It didn't occur to me that your vision of the sea is limited. This strip of land is called The Rubicon. Beyond it, there is a vast ocean littered with many beautiful islands and white sandy beaches. It is called the Deep Blue."

"Really? Ocean, beautiful islands and sandy beaches? My boss always told me there was no such thing as oceans, islands and beaches. He said they only exist in fairy tales."

"Of course there are! Only an autocratic boss would say there are no oceans and islands. Autocrats are compulsive liars. On the third day, the Maker created majestic oceans and idyllic islands with white beaches," swore the osprey as he placed his wings on his chest.

"Tell us, how do we get over there?"

"I don't have a clue. You're too heavy for me to lift with my talons."

"Yes. I'm too heavy for you," sighed Ventura.

"Once you cross The Rubicon, you can swim through the vast expanse of the ocean, in the same way I glide through the skies. Deep Blue merges with blue skies seamlessly in a *ying–yang* fashion. You can sing and dance as if there's no tomorrow. You can transform yourselves into devil-may-care thrill seekers. Or you can go with the flow - float and let the tidal waves carry you to no man's land. And you would have an added advantage ..."

"Really? What would that be?"

"Oh! You can dive and explore the depths of the ocean — where the mysteries are profound. I can't. I can only pick up the seashells on the seashores," reminded the osprey.

Applica, the younger and more impatient of the two, wanted to jump over the strip of land to get into Deep Blue.

"But we do not know how wide the strip is," cautioned Ventura.

"Let's ask the osprey," insisted Applica, looking at their friend.

Based on the information furnished by the osprey, they calculated they would be able to jump over the 150-foot Rubicon.

By vigorously flapping his tail to provide propulsion power and using his pectoral fins for steering, Applica accelerated to a breakneck speed of 25 miles per hour to gather enough momentum. Twenty feet from the strip of land, he leaped and somersaulted. He was very satisfied with his jump. He straightened his body to gain maximum speed. In mid-flight, he saw Deep Blue. It was vast and blue. He was very thrilled at the thought of diving into it.

Over-optimism was the architect of failure. Applica had overestimated his ability. Deep Blue was further than he thought.

Applica landed with a loud thud on the sandy grass patch. He failed to make it to the ocean. Like a crocodile, he tried to wriggle on the land to reach it. However, he was too heavy and clumsy. The land was uneven, interspersed with shrubs and rocks. Then, he saw an ugly sight — the skeletons and carcasses of dolphins who, like him, had failed in their endeavors. The graveyard was full of wannabes.

At this critical juncture, he came to realize his weakness, "Dolphins are not aware they are only mobile in water; they are useless on land. If only I could walk just a few feet, I would easily reach my destination alive."

The sun's rays were beating more intensely. Applica became weaker. The water on his body soon dried up. Breathing became difficult as he panted heavily. He struggled to move but could only shift his body by mere inches. He was fast losing his strength. Deep Blue was within his sight but it seemed miles beyond. Philosophizing to himself, he whispered the familiar saying, "So near, and yet so far."

Ventura heard haunting growls from Applica. The sounds grew fainter and fainter. There was nothing Ventura could do. He felt very sorry for his friend.

Soon, Applica reached his expiry date. On a sunny afternoon with punishing heat, he departed in a slow and agonizing death alone.

Being the wiser of the two, probably due to his age, Ventura reasoned it was risky for him to try to leap over The Rubicon. Life experiences had caused him to be risk-averse despite the fact that one must exploit chances when the probability of success was higher. Curiosity could reveal opportunities. And it was wise to be curious like children. Thus, he printed on the rocks:

Curiosity is the precursor to discovery.

VII

Ventura was excited by the thought of Deep Blue. For seven consecutive days, he swam along The Rubicon and surveyed every nook and cranny. He found nothing. He was convinced there would be a breakthrough if he persisted. A breakthrough was all he needed.

He harbored his dreams of frolicking in Deep Blue as it would present opportunities to career victims embroiled in mid-life crisis like him. In the Red Sea, there was bloodshed everywhere. Many career openings were closed to older executives like himself. Doors opened for the young, the educated and the connected. Employers preferred fresh graduates who were more energetic and were prepared to work harder and for longer hours for less pay. They were like clay, flexible to mold. Their minds were like sponges, ready to absorb information easily.

In the larger scheme of things, Ventura learned to look at the big picture. Look at the forest, not the trees - that was the mantra of the many MBA books he had read. After he was retrenched, he took time to appreciate the smaller things in life, things that had previously escaped his attention.

"There was beauty in small things. After all, the Maker had made all things beautiful. Big or small, He had made them all. If you looked at the forest too much, you missed the beauty of the trees, its twigs and the dew on the leaves. Only mindfulness made them visible."

He began to thank the Maker for all the creatures he had come across. Everyone, big or small, was important in the eyes of the Maker. Previously, he had been arrogant, being the prima donna in Dolphinarium. Hundreds of admirers applauded him when he performed death-defying stunts. He held the record for the highest and the most acrobatic twists and somersaults. After all those ego trips, he had to nibble at humble pie now. He scribbled:

In appreciation, clarity arose.

As he swam around appreciating the smaller things, he suddenly witnessed a shoal of small silvery-blue fish milling around at a corner. There were probably hundreds, if not thousands, of them. This was a phenomenon he had never seen before. Perhaps he had been too engrossed in other challenges that he had failed to observe the minute details. Where did they come from? He turned to the osprey whom he regarded as a mentor. Alas, the osprey pleaded ignorance.

Did the silvery-blue fish come from Deep Blue? Ventura swam along The Rubicon but did not see any opening. Puzzled, his mind was preoccupied with three questions — where did these fish come from? How could he cross over to the ocean? Were the two linked? If he could find the source of the fish, maybe he would discover the key to the secret passageway to Deep Blue! He knew he had to think out of the box and experience a paradigm shift. But how? All these years, he had worked at the same job, lived in the same old Red Sea, interacted with the same colleagues and hardened his habits. If he did the same things over and over, he would get the same results.

He remembered a quote from Einstein, "Insanity is the name of doing the same things over and over again and expecting different results."

To make it big, he realized he had to swim to uncharted waters — the ocean. This was where he would experience new products, new markets and exponential growth. Ventura knew that to think differently, he had to do things differently. To make it permanent, he put his thoughts in writing:

Breaking your routine is the first step to creativity.

He had been swimming in the daytime. What if he swam at night? Hmmm. So, one night, he risked a midnight dip. This was the first time in his life he had done something this crazy. He now recognized that craziness was one of the keys to creativity. Normally, at this time of night, he would be in deep slumber. He enjoyed his swim, although it was a bit quiet and eerie. The moon, hanging midway in the sky, was the only source of light. It looked like a painting hung on the wall. The sea was shimmering with reflected moonlight. The stars shone across the skies like diamonds sewn on a black stage curtain. The tide was low and the current slow. It was quiet and he was all alone.

He wrote:

It is only in the dark stars can shine.

As he was turning a tight corner of The Rubicon, he saw something he had not seen before. In the dim light, there appeared a small opening under The Rubicon, and water was flowing out. Using echolocation, he emitted high-frequency clicking sounds that bounced off the object and listened to the return echo. Yes, something was there. He located and worked out the shape of the opening. It was covered by water during high tide. No wonder he could not see it during the day. He should have used echolocation earlier but he rarely had the opportunity to use it in the well-provided and structured Dolphinarium. He glided towards it. It was pitch-black.

It was an underwater cave.

He was afraid to venture deeper into the cave as he could not see anything beyond eight feet. Failing to achieve further results, he called it a day.

Although he was tossing in his sleep, he dreamt that he ventured into Deep Blue to seek his fortune. As an immigrant in his newly-adopted country, he toiled for long hours. Despite both the xenophobic and ethnocentric environment, he assimilated fast and persevered to become a successful entrepreneur in marine services.

He self-talked, "Sweet dreams. Dreams are symbolic messages from the Maker. Dreams are free. It does not cost anything to dream. Dreams are light and they don't tie me down. With dreams, I will be able to fly. And it is good to dream. Dreams do come true. Many innovations have their origins in dreams."

Next day, Ventura woke up to a brand new day. He smiled to himself, readied to meet new challenges and cherished his dreams. He had a hunch there was something in the cave. Return he must to the cave to satisfy his curiosity. Dark though it might be, he knew he had to muster enough courage to enter the cave.

"Unless I have courage, I will never dare to try anything new," he thought. A courageous attempt was what he needed.

He retrieved his manual placed on his seminar altar and recalled what he had copied:

Results happen only when you try.
If you don't try, nothing will happen.

When you try, two things can happen.
You either succeed or you fail.
So, the chance of success is 50%.

Using auto-suggestion, he self-talked himself into the success of discovery. Equipped with a headlamp and some survival rations, he set forth on a new adventure — something he had never done before. For the first time, he was leaving his comfort zone for the unknown.

He reaffirmed his own philosophy: "Unless I lose sight of the shores of comfort, I can never explore the ocean of opportunities before my very eyes."

He thought about it and concluded that there were actually five zones:

Past Zone
Comfort Zone
Dead Zone
Opportunity Zone
Danger Zone

"The past zone has passed. There is no point regretting what you have done or not done. No amount of regret can alter the past. The present is the comfort zone where you feel safe and comfortable in your work and home. If you stay too long in the comfort zone, it will morph into a dead zone. If you dare leave the comfort zone, the opportunity zone awaits for you. But wait — do not wander too far. Otherwise, you may trip and fall into the danger zone."

AHA! There was a light bulb moment. He wrote:

O is for Opportunities
There is no Opportunity in yesterday
One Opportunity in Today
And Three Opportunities in Tomorrow

Uttering a prayer to the Maker for journey mercies, Ventura headed for the cave. At low tide, the entrance of the cave was noticeable. It was dark. He was frightened. Nevertheless, he chanted his mantra non-stop:

"Fear not. Fear not. Fear not."

With trepidation, he entered the cave. As he swam deeper into it, he felt an air of eeriness. There were sounds of water lapping against the walls. Focusing with his headlamp, the narrow and jagged cave walls appeared before his very eyes. The sides looked as if they were plastered with devilish gargoyles with water spouting out of their mouths, not unlike those in Gothic cathedrals. It was awful. It appeared as if they would spring and attack him at any moment. The water surface reflected spooky shadows in motion. Nevertheless, powered by his affirmations, he pressed on. He saw nothing but water and the black walls of the cave.

Then the cave dropped to a very steep descent and narrowed into a tunnel. Ventura was going deeper and deeper. It looked like a bottomless pit. He was doubtful where it would lead to or whether he would emerge alive. Trusting that his instinct would lead him to Deep Blue, he persevered. It was as black as coal. The water pressure increased. It was getting eerier.

Having second thoughts suddenly, he wanted to turn back. Why take risks and get injured, or worse, killed? What was at the end of the cave? Danger lurked in every corner. He continued, nevertheless. Trembling with fear, he was egged on by the spirit of discovery. There was a struggle within — FEAR versus DISCOVERY. He asked himself, "Should I quit before it's too late?" He remembered the concept of bailing out and cutting losses in his seminars.

He pondered,

"Would I do it if I had less fear?"

He noticed water was flowing out of the cave. He deduced there was an opening at the end of the cave. He persisted.

At the bottom, the tunnel spiraled upwards. He followed the passage obediently. There was barely enough space for a dolphin to squeeze through.

Suddenly, he saw a shimmering light. There was an opening at the end of the cave. He swam nearer. Yes, there was indeed light at the end of the proverbial tunnel. And it opened majestically into an awesome blue ocean, glittering like the sparkle of diamonds reflecting the full moon.

WOW! My Lord! The wonders and handiwork of the Maker!

He paused at the opening. He was dazzled. He was amazed. Like a young violinist playing to a full-house concert hall for his maiden performance, he stood in front of the vast ocean. His jaws were wide open. He was left speechless. He dared not venture any further. Never before had he seen such a vast expanse of water. Never had he witnessed a brighter and fuller moon. He turned back with his heart overwhelmed with awed wonder.

Ventura planned to return at the break of the next day when he could see more clearly. He could not sleep that night, tossing and turning every hour. He was fascinated by what he had seen and the vast opportunities Deep Blue presented to him.

The next day, he returned to the cave. Although it was covered with water, he had marked its precise location. He took a high leap and dived deep. He saw the cave entrance. As the water rushed in during high tide, he swam against the current. At the end of the cave, he surfaced. WOW! His jaw dropped. His eyes froze. The mighty pristine Deep Blue lay before him. This was the virgin ocean.

He yelled, "AWESOME! This is THE MIGHTY DEEP BLUE!"

He dashed into it. It was heavenly. The water was as refreshingly pristine as that from the Swiss Alps – a world of difference from the stale and polluted waters of the Red Sea. The air was as fresh as pine and the ocean was magnificently vast.

VIII

Ventura could not wait to tell Status Quo about his newfound discovery.

"I've uncovered a new marketplace with many opportunities," rattled off Ventura excitedly, gasping for another breath.

"Are you sure? I may not be wealthy but I'm pretty comfortable here," grumbled Status Quo doubtfully, almost drowning Ventura's enthusiasm.

"It's really exciting! I'm looking forward to exploring it!"

"At our age, we shouldn't risk new things, lest we break our bones!"

"We're not old. We're just experienced. Age is just a set of numbers. Let's discuss the degree of our spirit, not the numbers," persuaded Ventura.

"Don't kid yourself, Ventura."

"No. I'm not kidding. We should always prepare for second careers and reinvent ourselves continually," explained Ventura.

"I'm tired of looking around. I'll never get a better job."

"Never make a universal assumption 'Never'. Don't shut yourself from any opportunity. Come, allow me to take you to a paradise where opportunities abound — it's called Deep Blue."

"The water is always bluer on the other side."

"The water is bluer for those who nurture it."

"I'm sorry. I have no time," signed off Status Quo in a desperate attempt to kill the conversation.

"Those who have no time have only one job. Those who have time are entrepreneurs. Come, follow me and I shall make an entrepreneur out of you."

Status Quo refused stubbornly. She dared not risk leaving the comforts of the Red Sea, bloody though it might be. She accepted the realities and constraints of the Red Sea. For those who dared not risk, living in Deep Blue remained a mere pipe dream.

So Ventura went alone. He swam through the cave and emerged at Deep Blue. He leaped and frolicked and savored the crystal clear waters. He was a bit puzzled — the waters were actually greenish. Why was it called Deep Blue when the waters were lime green? Nevertheless, he executed numerous stunts that he was previously afraid to do. Never before had he felt so energetic and free.

From afar, Ventura saw the dorsal fin of another dolphin gliding towards him from behind. He was so delighted to see another of his kind in Deep Blue. It was accelerating at a speed faster than most dolphins. Wow! Dolphins in Deep Blue were better endowed.

Wait, was it a dolphin? Its dorsal fin was sharper than his. No, it was not a dolphin.

It was a shark.

Specifically, it was a great white shark. The predator was attacking him from behind so that it would not activate his echolocation.

Frozen by fear, Ventura panicked and swam for his life. The great white shark gave chase. It got nearer and nearer. Soon, it was just twelve feet away. Twelve feet separated life and death.

Ventura headed towards the cave. The great white shark lunged forward and bit into Ventura with its razor-sharp teeth. Ventura put up a violent struggle. He broke free, escaping with teeth marks on his body. In the nick of time, he accelerated and dived into the cave. As the cave entrance was too narrow for it to enter, the shark retreated.

Within the cave, Ventura trembled with fear as he recounted his near-death experience on his first unlucky day in Deep Blue. "This is not a Deep Blue. This is a bloody ocean!" he screamed in pain.

Blood was still trickling from his body as he remembered,

"In opportunities lie dangers."

Yet Deep Blue was too good to give up. "A winner must not quit," reaffirmed Ventura. He must try again. A fortnight later, after recuperating from his injury, he was raring to explore Deep Blue again.

"Come, Status Quo, join me in Deep Blue. It's beautiful out there," said Ventura, keeping her in the dark about the shark attack. Some things, he thought, were better left unsaid.

Due to Ventura's persistence, Status Quo changed her mind, "Okay. I'll give it a try. There's nothing to lose anyway."

Again, when they arrived, it was a beautiful ocean. They were refreshed by the pristine air, clear green waters and the wide open skies. This time, Ventura was more cautious and kept an open eye all the while for sharks. The two dolphins leaped and dived across the vast expanse of the mighty ocean. They arched their bodies, executing numerous circle flips. Using their echolocation, they spotted a shoal of bluefin tuna. They were thrilled. Being gregarious in nature, they wanted to make new friends. They chased the tuna. It was fun. The fresh and deep waters of Deep Blue offered less resistance and thus made their swimming swifter.

Just as they were about to catch up with the tuna, they crashed into an invisible wall. "Strange," Ventura thought for a second, "how can there be a wall in the ocean?"

But it was not a wall. It was a purse-seine net.

Unwittingly, they had swum into a drift net cast by two trawlers traveling at high speed to fish tuna. It was mounted with floats on top and sinkers at the bottom. They got entangled in the net, together with the bluefin tuna. This was the first time they had ever been trapped in a gigantic net.

Ventura got himself into a big mess again. He regretted his actions — he should not have pushed his luck too far. It was the price he paid for adventure.

There was no way out as the fishermen encircled them. The net was closing on them as the fishermen drew it tighter, just like drawing a purse string. It seemed like hours as they struggled in vain to escape. They panicked and burst into tears. There were flashbacks of painful memories. "This was how Mama and Papa were trapped and sold," sobbed Status Quo.

They surrendered. They were prepared for the net to close up and hoist them up when suddenly, they heard squeaks. Yes, squeaks from another dolphin.

"Remain calm and you'll be free," reassured the new dolphin as he consoled his two distressed newfound friends. "My name is Livita. I'm here to free you."

As Livita was outside the net, his overview of the escape route was clearer. Under his direction, the siblings maneuvered through several folds of the net. Then Livita instructed them to resurface to grasp some air and dive to the bottom of the ocean below the net. After several attempts, they found their way to freedom.

Even after the escape, Ventura still was trembling with shock and Status Quo remained in tears. They wanted to return to the Red Sea.

"I've never seen you two before. By the way, what are your names?" whistled Livita.

"I'm Ventura and she's Status Quo, my sister."

"Where do you come from?"

"The Red Sea."

"Oh. I've never heard of that place," exclaimed Livita curiously.

"It's a reclusive sea. The only access is through an underwater cave."

"That sounds interesting. I would love to see that place one day."

"Are you sure? It is small, restrictive and competitive. But it's safe, well organized and structured."

"Of course I'm keen. I want to experience every place in this world — the good, the bad and the ugly."

"We want to return to the Red Sea."

"Why?"

"First of all, I was nearly eaten by a great white shark and now we were nearly caught by fishermen."

Status Quo stared at Ventura. Judging from her horrified expression, Ventura knew his sister would never forgive him for not forewarning her of his near-death experience.

"Well, there's always danger lurking in every opportunity. You can't have clear blue skies all the time. Lightning and thunderstorms do pay you a visit from time to time. Take this as the tuition fee and be more careful next time," counseled Livita.

"What other dangers are there?" sobbed Ventura.

"You need to be aware of only the twin dangers — purse-seine nets and sharks. Dolphins are the favorite meal of tiger, bull and great white sharks," warned Livita.

"I love this big Deep Blue but it's fraught with danger."

"No. You've gotten it mixed up. This is Green Sea, not Deep Blue."

"Huh? This is not Deep Blue?" Ventura puzzled, realizing that the osprey had made a grave mistake.

"Yes. No sharks in the Deep Blue. Neither are there purse-seine nets. Please allow me to show you the way."

"No, I want to return to the Red Sea!" cried Status Quo, still crippled by residual fears.

Livita was athletic, charming and had a radiant complexion. It was love at first sight, although Status Quo didn't believe in it. She had fallen head over heels in love with him. However, fear took precedence over love.

"Let me lead you to Deep Blue first. Then you can decide."

Despite her infatuation, Status Quo was adamant about her decision. It was a confusing struggle within her. It was a battle between her head and her heart. Although she wanted to be with Ventura and Livita, she could not bear to leave the Red Sea. Eventually, she followed her head.

And so, the two friends accompanied Status Quo back to the Red Sea. She was contented living in her comfort zone, despite knowing that one day, her comfort zone would evolve into a dead zone.

IX

Ventura thought, "I can't be three times unlucky." So he consented and followed Livita to the Deep Blue. It was an hour's journey, 40 miles away.

Throwing caution to the wind, they swam aimlessly at breath-taking speed. There was no constraint or limit. They frolicked by diving in the ocean and leaping for joy into the air. They behaved like airplanes in mid-flight. They slapped their tails on the water surface and tail-walked. No one cared.

The ocean temperature was at a constant 63 degrees Fahrenheit — an ideal place for plankton to breed. This, in turn, attracted an abundance of aquatic animals — herring, cod and mackerel. They were the dolphins' favorite meals. Three-foot long jumbo flying fish and flying squid provided Livita and Ventura the opportunity to challenge each other's leaping and catching skills. Never did they suspect fish and squid could fly such long distances. Surely the day would come when dolphins could fly, too!

Far away on the horizon, Ventura saw the blue skies melting into the blue waters to create a *yin-yang* fusion. Suddenly, he froze for a second. Out of the horizon, a pod of about 15 dolphins appeared magically, leaping and diving in a choreographed fashion. Immediately, they swam towards the pair. Ventura was shocked. The dolphins were of different colors — pink, blue, purple and white! A lead dolphin swam ahead of the pod on a scouting mission, looking out for any unusual occurrences.

The pod greeted Livita and Ventura with great hospitality. Ventura observed that the other dolphins were more energetic and had higher EQ. He also realized their complexions were of a healthier glow, compared to his dull gray tone. Initially, he was a bit reserved. However, his newfound friends made him felt at home. Together, they had fun, executing new tricks and exploring new territories. It puzzled him how, in this pod, different types of dolphins — Atlantic spotted, Risso, striped and dusty, rough-toothed, short-finned pilot whales and false killer whales — co-existed in harmony as a closely-knit community. There was no jealousy, no rumor-mongering or "stab-you-in-the-back" mentality, unlike in the Red Sea.

Livita and Ventura enjoyed frolicking in the Deep Blue. They socialized with other dolphins and cruised leisurely for miles. Being playful creatures, they snapped their jaws and butted their heads against one another. They squeaked and whistled from their blowholes. Occasionally, they performed corralling — chasing sea bass, mackerel and tuna into the beach for fun and food. They engaged in fish-whacking – using their tails to hit smaller fish and throw them up in the air.

They dived deep to the ocean floor. Ventura had never seen such giant shrimps, squids, turtles, crabs and stingrays. Yummy! Never before had he tasted such quality epicurean seafood. He whistled with joy. He chased the giant squid at high speed as they jetted off using their propulsion system, squirting black ink to mask their escape. It thrilled him and he had a hearty laugh. The flower crabs at the ocean bed were eight meters wide! The sea turtles and stingrays were gracefully gigantic. Ventura had never witnessed such brilliant sea anemones before. Now, he appreciated the osprey's comment on how privileged he was – having the ability to explore the mysterious depths of the ocean.

He reflected, "Unless I leave the ponds, rivers and seas, I will not have arrived at the oceans."

As the dolphins explored, they saw a giant bluish-gray tail rising out of the ocean. Then, it swiftly disappeared. Ventura panicked. Another predator! Who said there were no sharks in the Deep Blue? Not again!

He fled for his life.

A Whale of Opportunities

"Take it easy. This is the blue whale, the largest mammal on the earth. At 106 feet long, it's larger than the prehistoric dinosaurs," explained Livita.

"That's colossal!"

"Although he can swallow you in a single gulp, he's totally harmless. Despite their looming size, blue whales are highly sociable creatures. This is a shining example of a humble and gentle giant!"

"Awesome!"

"The blue whale grows to its huge size by feeding on krill — tiny shrimp found in huge quantities on the ocean floor. You can achieve great things by doing small things daily."

"Wow! How compelling that is!" Ventura exclaimed as he made notes in his notebook, lest he forgot.

You can achieve great things by doing small things consistently.

"That's a good habit. 'The faintest ink is more powerful than the most retentive memory' was quoted by Confucius frequently."

"Haha! Another stimulating quotation!"

The faintest ink is more powerful than the most retentive memory.

The blue whale greeted them by spraying water out of its blowhole. Then it dived into the depths of the ocean by saluting its tail in the air. Livita and Ventura tried to mimic its actions. True to the expression, they had a whale of a time indeed.

Out on the horizon, Ventura spotted some coconut trees.

"What is this? It's heavenly."

"It's called an island."

"Wow! It's fascinating! This is the first time I've ever seen an island!"

The idyllic island was lined with swaying coconut trees and golden sand. The blue waves gently lapped the beaches, creating a picturesque postcard scenery. Exotic corals lay below the crystal clear waters. Herons and other migratory egrets hovered above the colorful flowering plants. The trees were abundantly luscious and green. It was a paradise.

Now he could verify the truth the eagle had told him about oceans and islands. His former boss at Dolphinarium had lied through his teeth - all to restrain him from seeking greener pastures when he was at his prime.

On the eastern end of the island was a beautiful ring-shaped atoll reef. Within it was a serene water inlet. Pretty pink flamingos basked in the sun. Livita and Ventura leaped into its sparkling waters. It was comforting and relaxing.

"Guess. What is this called?" asked Livita.

"I don't know."

"This is the Blue Lagoon. It's the pinnacle of the Deep Blue. There's a scenic waterfall towards the end. This is where dolphins come for their three R's."

"Pardon me. What are the 3 R's?"

"Rejuvenate, Renew and Reinvent."

Ventura thought if such a spa had been available in Dolphinarium, his career life-cycle could have been prolonged. He would not have burnt out so early.

At the northern end of the island, appearing out of a rocky out-crop, was a tall, white cylindrical building.

"And what is that?" asked Ventura.

"That is a lighthouse. It shines a powerful beam of light at night to give direction to those lost in the ocean. It also marks hazardous coastlines."

"How I wish there had been an angel to guide me when I was a hot-headed young man," said Ventura whimsically. He thought to himself, "When I become successful, I'll return to society by coaching and mentoring the youth."

"It's cylindrical to reduce the effect of the gale on tall structures."

"Yes. I understand now."

"You must construct structures in alignment with, and not against, the elements of *fengshui* — wood, fire, earth, metal and water. You can't fight against the forces of nature."

As they swam towards the western part of the island, they saw a school of dolphins diving into the Deep Blue.

"What are they doing there?" asked Ventura.

"They are hunting for oysters."

"Oysters? They eat oysters?"

"No. They are harvesting pearls in the oysters."

"What are pearls?"

"They are beautiful, white, round, naturally-formed gemstones made into rings, earrings and necklaces."

"Oh! In the Red Sea, I've seen my rich ladies wearing them," recalled Ventura. "I must starting looking for oysters myself."

"Many think that every oyster has a pearl inside."

"Is that not so?"

"Not all oysters have pearls inside. Most don't. There is no guarantee that when you find an oyster, a pearl lies within. It's just like there's no guarantee in life; only opportunity."

"Great learning point."

"The birth of a pearl is miraculous. Gemstones have to be mined from the earth. They must be cut and polished to reflect their beauty. But pearls are formed naturally from within."

"Really? How?"

"A foreign object, like sand, gets into the oyster accidentally. As the oyster gets irritated, it tries to expel the sand. When it fails to eject this irritation and to protect itself, the body will secrete a smooth crystalline substance over the irritant. Layer by layer, it will continue to secrete the same substance that creates the shell. After a period, the foreign object will be encased by a silky and brilliant crystalline coating. A miracle, called a pearl, is formed. When there are constant irritations and pressures, miracles do happen."

Ventura listened intently.

"It's only in clean waters where you can find pearls in oysters. Our black pearls, indigenous to the South Pacific, are the roundest and the rarest. They can reflect light to form a rainbow. Pearls that are found naturally are more valuable than those farmed where they slit the oysters and insert a grain of sand. The bigger the oyster, the bigger the pearl you can find. No oyster is willing to surrender its pearl just like no one will give up his prized assets. You have to insert a knife into its opening between the shells and twist to prise it open."

Livita continued, "The cultivation of pearls is a timely reminder that what seemingly looks like an overnight success actually takes years of consistency and hard work peppered with risk.

We recognize that life is imperfect. Finding a pearl requires a combination of hard work, persistence and good luck. Some are successful in finding pearls without much diligence. Some try different things at different times before they discover their pearl – their fortune. Others never find the pearl, settling for the meat and the shell instead.

There are many obstacles and failures. With each encounter, we develop a learning experience. There's no failure; only success delayed. Over a period of trials and tribulation, we become hardened and pearls of wisdom are born. There are no shortcuts to success. Success is a continuous journey, not a final destination."

Ventura got his epiphany.

"*Terra es mea ocystae,*" quoted Livita.

"That sounds Greek to me!"

"The world's my oyster – in Latin," Livita explained. "Make the world your oyster too."

There was a pregnant pause. Ventura's face was wrinkled with doubt.

"The world's your oyster. Healthy young man, the world is holding a great treasure for you. Opportunities await you and all you have to do is grasp them. You have the ability to do anything you want and the freedom to go anywhere you choose. Your time is limited. Do things you have a passion for and have passion for the things you do. Then your work will be a joyful flow. Do not do things just to please others. You'll end up being unhappy," exhorted Livita. "Find the oyster. Harvest the pearl. Make the world your oyster! "

"Wow! Thanks for the inspiration."

"*Carpe diem.*"

"Pardon me."

"It's Latin again. *Carpe diem* - Seize the day."

Lest he forgot the new Latin proverbs, Ventura quickly jotted them down in his notebook.

Terra es mea ocystae
The World's My Oyster

Carpe Diem
Seize the Day

Ventura pondered deeply over the exhortation:

"Make the world your Oyster!"

X

Ventura was determined to find his oysters and harvest the pearls within.

As he ventured further in the Deep Blue, he realized there were tremendous opportunities, totally untapped, in this virgin ocean.

One morning, while cruising in the Deep Blue, there was a distress call from a yacht. Ventura went to the rescue. A fiery storm had wrecked the mast and torn the sails earlier in the Green Sea. As the engine had stalled, the captain and three crew members were stuck in the middle of the ocean. They needed help. If not for Ventura, who happened to hear the distress call, they would have had to wait for hours for assistance from passing vessels. Ventura assured them he would seek help.

He sped to the Port Police and reported the incident. Then he accompanied them in their speedboat to rescue the yacht. The crew thanked Ventura profusely. In recognition of his public-spiritedness, he was awarded the St Micah's Cross.

Ventura then realized there were tremendous opportunities in Deep Blue that could be commercialized. One immediate business was a patrol and rescue service to help stranded surfers, fishing boats, yachts and commercial vessels. Thus, he launched Blue Lagoon Patrol. There were no competitors. No one else had exploited this market – to provide rescue services to ocean users.

He started as a solo patrol officer. His first job involved getting medicine for a sickly boy in a fishing boat. Word-of-mouth marketing soon leapfrogged his business. Response was so overwhelming that he could not cope. Soon, he recruited another dolphin to assist him. In less than six months, he had a task force of five dolphin patrol and rescue officers. The dolphins were also engaged to rescue injured scuba divers and bring them up to the surface.

Blue Lagoon Patrol's strategy was to rely on manual labor and personalized service, as even the best technology and electronics could fail at any time. There were numerous requests for Blue Lagoon Patrol to provide guide services. Many yachts and fishing boats new to the Deep Blue got lost in their navigation while attempting to reach their destination.

Ventura envisioned there was indeed a market for guide services. So he formed a subsidiary, Blue Lagoon Vision Guides. It was responsible for escorting big ocean liners and tankers safely into the harbor. Pleasure crafts and boats also sought their services to guide them quickly and safely through the reefs. Soon, he had a staff strength of 11 guides.

Business prospered. Before long, Blue Lagoon Patrol and Blue Lagoon Vision Guides expanded quickly as there were virtually no competitors. Again, Ventura had opened up a brand new market.

One day, the dolphin saw a flotilla of gray ships engaging in a host of activities. They were, in fact, military ships — an aircraft carrier, a minesweeper, destroyers and supply ships.

He spoke to the captain of a ship, "Hi! What are you all doing here? Having a celebration or a mutiny?"

"We're conducting a military exercise," replied the Rear Admiral of the Asia Pacific Navy. "By the way, who are you?"

"Ventura is my name. I'm a dolphin."

"Oh. I thought you were a talking gray mini-submarine."

"What are all these ships?" inquired Ventura inquisitively.

"The center big ship, which is the biggest of all, is the aircraft carrier. It is supported by two supply ships, three destroyers and a minesweeper."

"Pardon my ignorance. What's a minesweeper?"

"A minesweeper detects and clears all the mines planted in the sea."

"Oh! I can do that easily, swiftly and inexpensively for you."

Immediately, another business opportunity sprang up in his mind. He could organize a team of dolphins to locate booby traps and detect mines. The next day, he registered a company, Blue Lagoon Military Services.

He proposed to the Rear Admiral to outsource the search for booby traps and mine clearing to Blue Lagoon Military Services at a fraction of their present cost. A tender was called for and Blue Lagoon won the bid hands down as there were no other genuine bidders. Their mine detection and clearing services were so effective that the Navy commissioned a study to decommission the minesweepers.

In wartime, the Navy used Blue Lagoon Military Services to detect, mark and disable underwater dangers like mines, enemy divers, ships and submarines. The Navy fit dolphins with equipment that amplified their natural sonar pulses and relayed them back to Navy Intelligence. Dolphins were hard to detect with radar and sonar. Even when they were detected, enemies dismissed them as harmless sea creatures.

Ventura's first dramatic encounter with the humble gentle giant, the blue whale, had left him with deep impressions. So, he formed a whale-watching company, WWW (Wild Whale Watchers), to guide tourists to observe wild whales ranging from 11-foot pygmy whales to the 98-foot blue whale. With a life span of up to 100 years, whales are highly intelligent and social animals, travelling in groups called pods. Pollution, whaling, aquarium capture and a reduction of food supply had taken a toll on them. These expeditions educated the public and corrected the mistaken impressions that many people harbored about them.

Knowing that dolphins were friendly and comforting mammals, Ventura pioneered flipper-therapy, a form of AAT (Animal-Assisted Therapy). This was a very effective treatment for depression in which depressed patients spent time playing and caring for dolphins. It helped them to adhere to a daily schedule. The therapy reduced the patients' loneliness and anxiety while increasing their self-esteem. This form of therapy also helped improve autism amongst children.

Ventura's enterprise grew at such an enormous pace that he listed all his companies under the flagship of Blue Lagoon Management in the New Workland Stock Exchange.

Although Blue Lagoon Management made huge profits, it did not neglect its corporate social responsibility (CSR). Determined to be good corporate citizen, it launched its CSR programs. Its staff helped to direct stranded whales who had beached themselves on the coast back to the ocean. Whales were navigated by the earth's magnetic fields. When these fields were disrupted, their sonar could not detect a sloping sandy beach. And by the time they realized it was a beach, it was already too late.

Ventura's company also freed both dolphins and whales captured by fishermen by biting away the ropes to free them. They assisted other fishermen by driving fish towards them. At other times, they drove fish to shallow waters and rolled over, allowing fishermen to throw in their nets.

For his business and social entrepreneurship, Ventura was award-ed the St. Santiago Cross.

Once back to the Blue Lagoon, he relaxed.

This was where he could empty his thoughts to recharge. He had to find more oysters and harvest the pearls.

"The world's my oyster," he smiled to himself. He repeated in Latin,

"*Terra es mea ocystae.*"

The End

Exercises

To derive maximum benefits from reading and applying this book's principles, do the following exercises. You can either answer them individually or as a company.

Vision and Mission

What is your company's vision?

A vision is a general picture of where your company wants to go and what your company wants to achieve ultimately.

Where do you see yourself in 3, 5 and 10 years' time?

What is your company's mission?

A mission states why your company wants to achieve its vision. It also specifies the business you are in and the customers you serve.

What are your company's corporate values?

Dreams

What did you want to be when you were a child?

What did you want to be when you were a teenager?

What are you doing now?

If you could go back in time now and speak to yourself when you were a young person, what would you say to him or her?

Significant Areas

What is your USP (Unique Selling Proposition)?

In other words, what is so unique about your products/services that customers are eager to buy them?

Who are your competitors?

(Know thy enemies and know thyself. A hundred battles won. Sun Tze)

What is your KPI (Key Performance Index)?

In other words, what are the important areas in your work by which your performance is measured?

Self-Motivation

What are the daily affirmations you say to yourself?

If you could develop yourself to your fullest potential, describe how you would transform yourself.

List your favorite mottoes or slogans.

(It's ideal if you can coin one yourself.)

Time Management

List your daily schedule.

What are the routines that bore you (those that you want to break)?

What are your weekly goals?

What are your monthly goals?

What are your goals for this year?

What is one single goal, which when achieved, would make a big difference in your life?

What are the things you need to do to achieve your goals?

How does your three-year plan look like?

Unfulfilled Goals

What are some of the things you have procrastinated over which should have been completed?

What prevented you from achieving the goals?

(List behavior, time-competing activities, etc.)

What were your other commitments?

What were your assumptions that were wrong?

Plan B
What is your Plan B?

(If what you are doing now is terminated or fails, what is your next plan?)

What are the driving forces that would push you to execute Plan B?

What are the restraining forces that would prevent you from executing Plan B?

Self-Development
What are the courses you have attended?

What have you learned and applied from these courses?

What are the courses you plan to attend? When?

How will they benefit you?

What commitments (plans, time reservation, savings, etc) have you made to attend these courses?

Personal Assessment
Who drives the bus of your life?

List all your limiting beliefs.

List the events for which you are the cause.

List the events in which you are the effect.

List the events where what you perceived in your mind was projected to other people.

List your top three wishes:

If only...

If only...

If only...

Uncertainties

What are your fears?

What are your worries?

What are the things you thought might go wrong that actually went wrong subsequently (Murphy's Law)?

What would you have achieved if there were no fears or worries?

Failure

What were the occasions in which you have failed?

What were the things you have started on but quit halfway?

List the occasions when you were over-optimistic.

List the things you failed to appreciate which later turned out to be important.

What would you have achieved if you knew you wouldn't fail?

Comfort Zone

What are your shores of comfort, where you feel very comfortable in what you are doing?

What are the oceans of opportunities you want to explore?

What are the things you want to do but dare not?

The Herd Instinct

What were the occasions when you followed the masses?

What were the occasions when you were the lone ranger and went contrary to the masses?

Live the Dream

If you are free to dream, what are your dreams?

If you have more courage, what new things would you try?

What are the things you would like to try where there would be nothing to lose in trying?

What are the things you are curious about?

List the occasions you closed your mind to opportunities.

Your Heart and Your Head

What are the things you have a passion for?

These are the things you have feelings for.

What are the things you have a head for?

These are the things you can do well and with ease.

What are the things you have both passion and a head for?

Summary

Part 1 — Crafting Strategy

Define your product(s) or service(s).

Identify the business that you are in.

List the unique benefits of your product(s) or service(s) which your competitors do not have. This is your competitive advantage.

Identify all the Deep Blue markets that are available.

Where are your oysters? Target the Deep Blue market you want to enter.

List any opportunities available in the Deep Blue.

List the benefits of your product(s) or service(s) that are lacking in the Deep Blue.

List how these benefits can be of value to your customers.

Think about the additional benefits you can add to your product(s) or service(s) from your resources, capability, core competencies and supply chain.

Recognize your weaknesses and work out a plan to eliminate them.

Craft a vision and mission statement.

Destroy all your self-limiting beliefs.

Devise a strategy for entering the Deep Blue.

Devise a strategy for maintaining your presence in the Deep Blue.

Craft a battle cry for your company, product(s) or service(s).

Part 2 – Attacking the Deep Blue

Identify three of your closest competitors.

- What are their strengths?
- What are their weaknesses?

Devise a plan to market your products.

Take massive action to activate and realize your plan.

Monitor your progress periodically.

If there are deviations, take remedial action to stay on course.

Keep up the momentum in the Deep Blue.

Continually reinvent your product(s) or service(s) and scout for new Deep Blue.

The Author

Michael Lum, author of *Who Broke My Rice Bowl?*, *I Once Wore Diapers*, and *From Beggars to Millionaires*, lives in Singapore and has over twenty years of experience as a business coach.

A master trainer for his corporate training company, HardKnocksCollege, Lum also instructs at Nanyang Technological University and for the Institute of Singapore Chartered Accountants and the Marketing Institute of Singapore. He also lectures on business strategy and negotiation at SIM University.

In addition to holding a bachelor of accountancy, a master of commerce, and a graduate diploma in training and development, Lum is also a certified trainer with the American Board of NLP and the American Management Association. In addition, he is an ICF-certified coach and a Louis Allen program leader.

In 2003, he was recognized as the ABC True Hero for his efforts to better the lives of retrenched workers.

Website: www.HardKnocksCollege.com
Email: MikeLum@HardKnocksCollege.com

Make The World Your Oyster!

shows you how to

- Anticipate change
- Have courage to leave your comfort zone
- Venture to new market
- Embrace change

"Make The World Your Oyster! is an illuminating business parable about two dolphins who are mid-life executives. As their products reach the end of the life cycle, they ponder their situation. In the quest for solutions, they have a series of adventures containing both surprise and wisdom.

Michael Lum is a consummate storyteller whom I have known for some time. He is passionate about his work and the role of stories as teaching tools. This parable reflects precisely the realities of today's corporate world to which we must respond or be left behind. As you read this book, put yourself in the story and consider the decisions you have to make and the consequences of those decisions. Used in the right way, this book will guide you out of your comfort zone and into the innovation zone.

Make the world your oyster! Go and search for the pearl."

Stephen C. Lundin, Ph.D
Author of the five million copy best-selling: FISH!
Author, FISH! Sticks, FISH! Tales, FISH for Life,
Top Performer, Loops, CATS and Ubuntu

www.ingramcontent.com/pod-product-compliance
Lightning Source LLC
Chambersburg PA
CBHW021437170526
45164CB00001B/273